Survival Guides You Didn't Know You Needed

SURVIVING A BIGFOOT ATTACK

Thomas Kingsley Troupe

BLACK RABBIT BOOKS

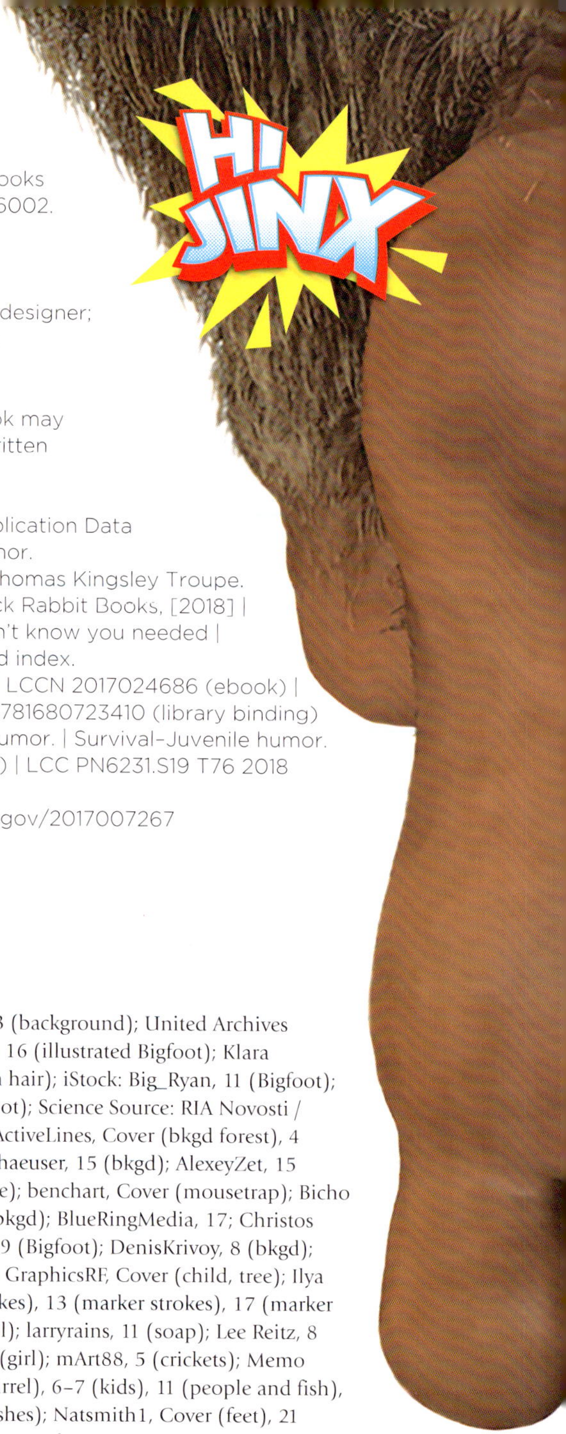

Hi Jinx is published by Black Rabbit Books
P.O. Box 3263, Mankato, Minnesota, 56002.
www.blackrabbitbooks.com

Marysa Storm, editor; Michael Sellner, designer;
Catherine Cates, production designer;
Omay Ayres, photo researcher

Library of Congress Cataloging-in-Publication Data
Names: Troupe, Thomas Kingsley, author.
Title: Surviving a bigfoot attack / by Thomas Kingsley Troupe.
Description: Mankato, Minnesota : Black Rabbit Books, [2018] | Series: Hi jinx. Survival guides you didn't know you needed | Includes bibliographical references and index.
Identifiers: LCCN 2017007267 (print) | LCCN 2017024686 (ebook) | ISBN9781680723717 (e-book) | ISBN 9781680723410 (library binding)
Subjects: LCSH: Sasquatch–Juvenile humor. | Survival–Juvenile humor.
Classification: LCC PN6231.S19 (ebook) | LCC PN6231.S19 T76 2018 (print) | DDC 818/.602-dc23
LC record available at https://lccn.loc.gov/2017007267

Printed in China. 9/17

Image Credits

Alamy: Handout, 12 (Bigfoot); John Zada, 3 (background); United Archives GmbH, 1, 20; Dreamstime: Donald Purcell, 16 (illustrated Bigfoot); Klara Viskova; 12 (child), Terriana, 18–19 (brown hair); iStock: Big_Ryan, 11 (Bigfoot); memoangeles, 7 (Bigfoot); retoid, 15 (Bigfoot); Science Source: RIA Novosti / Sputnik, 16 (Bigfoot photo); Shutterstock: ActiveLines, Cover (bkgd forest), 4 (bkgd), 7 (bkgd), 16 (bkgd); Adrian Niederhaeuser, 15 (bkgd); AlexeyZet, 15 (child); Arcady, 3 (note), 10 (note), 18 (note); benchart, Cover (mousetrap); Bicho Vega, 19 (child); blue67sign, 11 (dock and bkgd); BlueRingMedia, 17; Christos Georghiou, 4 (torn paper); dedMazay, 18–19 (Bigfoot); DenisKrivoy, 8 (bkgd); frescomovie, Back Cover, (bkgd), 11 (bkgd); GraphicsRF, Cover (child, tree); Ilya Chalyuk, 5 (marker strokes), 9 (marker strokes), 13 (marker strokes), 17 (marker strokes), 20 (marker strokes); irin-k, 14 (ball); larryrains, 11 (soap); Lee Reitz, 8 (pushpins on ground); Lorelyn Medina, 16 (girl); mArt88, 5 (crickets); Memo Angeles, Cover, (kids), 4–5 (bunny), 5 (squirrel), 6–7 (kids), 11 (people and fish), Morphart Creation, 16 (man); MSSA, 5 (bushes); Natsmith1, Cover (feet), 21 (feet); opicobello, 8 (bottom); Pasko Maksim, Back Cover, (top), 14 (torn corner), 23 (torn edge), 24 (torn edge); Pitju, 21 (edge); RikoBest, Cover (bkgd Bigfoot), 3–4 (foot), 8 (foot), 23 (Bigfoot); Rob Hainer, 18–19 (apron); sirius1, 16 (photo frame); SlipFloat, 6 (footprint), 21 (footprints); SofiaPink, 12 (curlers); totallypic, 18 (arrows); Ultrashock, 8 (pins in foot); unknown, 4 (chicken); Yoko Design, 18–19 (hair on Bigfoot) Every effort has been made to contact copyright holders for material reproduced in this book. Any omissions will be rectified in subsequent printings if notice is given to the publisher.

CONTENTS

CHAPTER 1
A Camping Trip Gone Wrong. 5

CHAPTER 2
Run for the Hills. 9

CHAPTER 3
Gifts for the Giant. . . .13

CHAPTER 4
Fight for Your Life. 17

CHAPTER 5
Get in on the Hi Jinx. .20

Other Resources. 22

Dear Reader,

To be honest, the author's **manuscript** wasn't supposed to become a book. There was a horrible mix up. You can keep reading, if you want. Just don't take any of these suggestions seriously.

Sincerely,
a very sorry editor

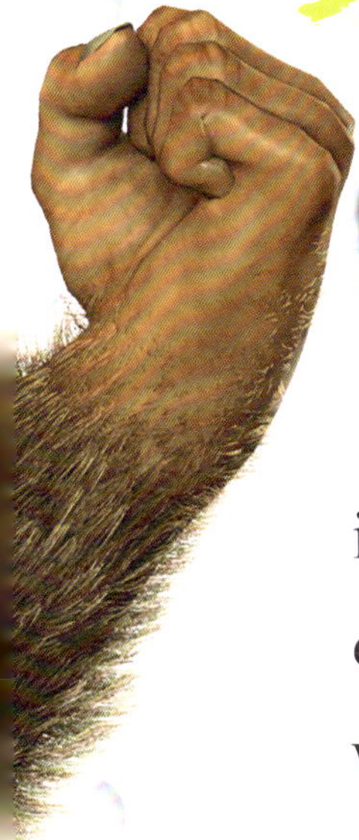

Chapter 1 A CAMPING TRIP GONE WRONG

There's nothing quite like camping in the great outdoors! Nature is on full display. Forest creatures **frolic** in the woods. Crickets sing their songs at night.

But then something growls in the distance. The ground shakes as the creature begins to run. A hairy giant emerges from the trees. It could happen, you know. A Bigfoot can attack at any time!*

*Editor's Note: No. No, it cannot.

Time to Survive!

The monster roars at full volume. It throws things around. It won't be long until the Bigfoot squashes everyone. Those giant feet are deadly.

Thankfully, you're prepared. You've got a survival guide you never thought you'd need. It's time to survive a Bigfoot attack!

Top Five Places Where a Bigfoot Will Find YOU

Washington (629 sightings)
California (436 sightings)
Florida (310 sightings)
Illinois (284 sightings)
Ohio (268 sightings)

as of June 2017

Survival List

Things that Will Slow Down a Bigfoot

building blocks
mousetraps
uncooked macaroni

Chapter 2
RUN FOR THE HILLS

The best way to survive an attack is to leave the forest! Outrunning a Bigfoot isn't easy, though. You will need help.

You probably think you know what you need for a camping trip. Just some sleeping bags, flashlights, and food, right? Wrong. Whenever there's a risk of a Bigfoot attack, bring tacks. Pack at least five boxes.

A Bigfoot's most famous feature is also its greatest weakness. A Bigfoot doesn't wear shoes. That means its huge feet are perfect targets. Sprinkle tacks behind you as you run away. Then listen to the howls!

Head for Water

Bigfoot monsters stink! These hairy **fiends** smell like a loaded port-a-potty.*

Like garlic keeps away a vampire, baths **repel** a Bigfoot. Head for the nearest lake or stream. And don't forget the soap. Bigfoot monsters would rather flee than wash up.

Survival List

Some of the All-Time Worst Smells

a Bigfoot's armpits
sunbaked vomit
dumpster juice

*Editor's Note: I'm very sorry if this makes you want to vomit. If you do throw up, it's best to clean it up right away.

Survival List

Things To Use as Makeshift Combs

(In case you forgot to bring one.)

pinecones
sticks
your fingers
plastic sporks

Chapter 3 GIFTS FOR THE GIANT

Why is that Bigfoot so angry? Well, it *is* covered in hair. Imagine if you had hair all over your face. You might be angry too. A simple gift could brighten the Bigfoot's mood.

Give a comb to the Bigfoot as a peace offering. If it calms down, gently comb its hair. Carefully clear hair from its eyes. Be careful not to hit a **snarl**. Bigfoot will growl at you!

Soccer Ball

Maybe the Bigfoot is just bored. It has big feet and nothing to do with them.

Why not bring a soccer ball to play with? Give the Bigfoot a quick lesson. It'll be kicking the ball like a pro in no time. Just be sure to let it win, OK?

Survival List

A Bigfoot doesn't like being called "Bigfoot." Try out some cool nicknames.

Harry
(Hairy works too.)
BFB
(Big Furious Bigfoot)
Sassy
(Short for Sasquatch.)

Many photos of Bigfoot creatures have been taken. Most of them have been proven fake.

Chapter 4 FIGHT FOR YOUR LIFE

Some Bigfoot monsters won't play games or let you near their hair. In that case, it's time to fight back. Want to scare off a Bigfoot? Use a camera!

You know how much you hate kidney beans? Bigfoot monsters feel the same way about cameras. They hate them! Whenever someone tries to take a Bigfoot's picture, the monster turns and runs.*

**Editor's Note: Well, the author does have a point here.*

Haircuts

Sometimes, you have to hit Bigfoot where it hurts. Its hair! A Bigfoot likes getting its hair combed, but it really hates haircuts.

Set up a barbershop in the forest! Lead your hairy customer to it. When the Bigfoot sees the scissors, it'll head for the hills!

Survival List

Top Hairstyles for a Bigfoot

- buzz cut
- Mohawk
- man bun

(or woman bun for the lady Bigfoot in your life)

You never know when you'll run into a Bigfoot. They're big, smelly, and they throw **boulders** at you. Just keep this trusty guide at your side. The Bigfoot monsters will be the ones taking a hike.

Chapter 5
GET IN ON THE HI JINX

Many people don't think Bigfoot creatures are real. But other people are believers. In fact, the hunt for Bigfoot creatures is popular. *Finding Bigfoot* is a TV show about a team searching for the creatures. So far, the creatures won't stop and pose for a good picture. But the hunt continues. Believers are certain the creature is out there!

Take It One Step More

1. Do you believe in Bigfoot creatures? Do some research to help you decide.

2. People struggle to take pictures of Bigfoot creatures. Why do you think it's hard to get a photo?

3. What do you think the author of this book was thinking? If his suggestions are crazy, why did he write the book?

GLOSSARY

boulder (BOHL-der)—a very large rounded piece of rock

fiend (FEEND)—a very evil or cruel person or creature

frolic (FROL-ik)—to play and move about happily

manuscript (MAN-yuh-skript)—the original copy of a book before it has been printed

repel (ri-PEL)—to force an enemy or attacker to stop an attack and turn away

snarl (SNAHRL)—a tangle usually of hairs or thread

LEARN MORE

BOOKS

Loh-Hagan, Virginia. *Bigfoot: Magic, Myth, and Mystery.* Magic, Myth, and Mystery. Ann Arbor, MI: Cherry Lake Publishing, 2017.

Noll, Elizabeth. *Bigfoot.* Strange … But True? Mankato, MN: Black Rabbit Books, 2017.

Perish, Patrick. *Is Bigfoot Real?* Unexplained, What's the Evidence? Mankato, MN: Amicus, 2014.

WEBSITES

Bigfoot Facts
softschools.com/facts/general/bigfoot_facts/1195/

Finding Bigfoot
discoverykids.com/games/finding-bigfoot/

Sasquatch – Our Furry Friends?
www.cbc.ca/kidscbc2/the-feed/sasquatch-our-furry-friends

INDEX

B

Bigfoot features

  feet, 6, 9, 14

  hair, 5, 13, 18

  smell, 10, 19

Bigfoot hunters, 20

C

camping, 5, 9

P

photos, 16, 17, 20, 21

S

sightings, 6